better together*

*This book is best read together, grownup and kid.

a kids book about

a kids book about FEMINISM

by Emma Mcilroy

A Kids Co.
Editor and Designer Jelani Memory
Creative Director Rick DeLucco
Studio Manager Kenya Feldes
Sales Director Melanie Wilkins
Head of Books Jennifer Goldstein
CEO and Founder Jelani Memory

DK
Editor Emma Roberts
Senior Production Editor Jennifer Murray
Senior Production Controller Louise Minihane
Senior Acquisitions Editor Katy Flint
Managing Art Editor Vicky Short
Publishing Director Mark Searle
DK would like to thank Natasha Devon

This American Edition, 2024
Published in the United States by DK Publishing
1745 Broadway, 20th Floor, New York, NY 10019

DK, a Division of Penguin Random House LLC
Cover design by Jonathan Simcoe

23 24 25 26 27 10 9 8 7 6 5 4 3 2 1
001-339150-Feb/2024

Published in Great Britain by Dorling Kindersley Limited.

A catalog record for this book is available from the Library of Congress.
ISBN: 978-0-7440-9464-0

Printed and bound in China

www.dk.com

akidsco.com

This book was made with Forest Stewardship Council™ certified paper - one small step in DK's commitment to a sustainable future.
For more information go to www.dk.com/our-green-pledge

For Caroline, Daniel & John—
may the future be feminist.

Intro
for grownups

When you hear a little boy say, "Boys are better than girls," it's more than just a frivolous statement. We are so conditioned to sexism that we sometimes forget it exists at all or act like it's harmless. It's not.

So how do we change this?

Believe it or not, feminism is the answer. I know—the "f-word" can sound intimidating. But this book is on a mission to make feminism not only accessible to every kid, regardless of gender, but also something they aspire to embrace.

Buckle up, and hopefully by the end of this book, you'll call yourself a feminist, too!

Hi, my name is Emma.

I'm from Belfast, a city in the top part of Northern Ireland.

I'm a CEO.*

*CEO stands for Chief Executive Officer.
It's a fancy way of saying "the boss"!

I'm a woman.

And I’m a feminist.

Feminism is

SUPER COOL.

And guess what?

You can be a feminist, too.

And if you choose to be one,

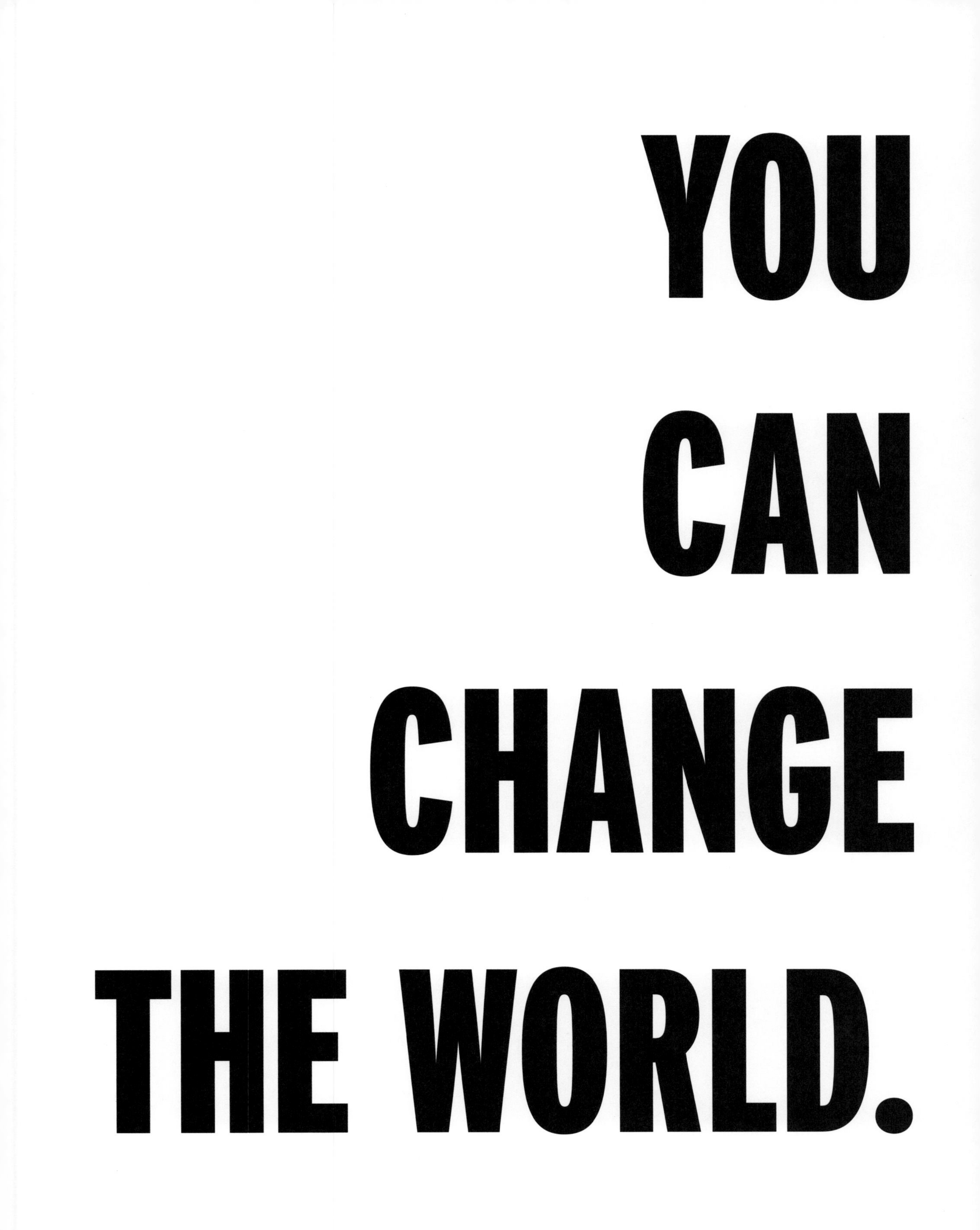
YOU
CAN
CHANGE
THE WORLD.

Some people think feminism is scary.

Some people think only women or girls can be feminists.

Some people think feminists don't like men or boys.

But that’s not true.

Feminism is the belief that...

EVERYONE IS EQUAL, NO MATTER WHAT THEIR GENDER IS.

1.

Feminists believe people should be able to choose what they want to do and how they want to be.

2.

Feminists believe that just because you're a girl, it doesn't mean you are less valuable.

3.

Feminists believe everybody should have the same opportunities.

4.

Feminists want the world to be a better place for everyone.

DO YOU AGREE?

Sometimes people treat girls differently...

Right?

Some people think girls...

can't do math.

aren't good at science.

should be thin.

should always look pretty.

can't be doctors.

have to get married.

should make less money.

Some people think boys are...

better.
stronger.
smarter.
faster.
more capable.

But...

THAT'S NO

ONSENSE!

Let me tell you the...

TRUTH!

GIRLS CAN WIN THE WORLD CUP!

Just ask Megan Rapinoe.

GIRLS CAN RUN BIG COMPANIES!

Like PepsiCo—ever heard of Pepsi?

GIRLS CAN WIN NOBEL PRIZES!

Like Malala, at 17 years old.

GIRLS

CAN

BE

PRESIDENT!

Like in Ireland.

EVEN IF YOU'R

E NOT A GIRL.

Because there are so many things that have to...

NGE.

Like when you hear someone say...

That's not for girls...

Girls can't...

Boys are better at...

Remember, that's NOT TRUE!

And tell them that you know of a girl who...

WON THE
NOBEL PRIZE!

And if you're a girl...

BE

ACCEPT

LOVE

APPRECIATE

YOURSELF.

YOURSELF.

YOURSELF.

YOURSELF.

Because you're

OME!!

I’m a feminist, and I want to fight for all women and girls...

NO MATTER...

what their skin color is.

which country they're from.

who they choose to love.

what body parts they have.

how much money they make.

what they choose to wear.

Because when we fight for every woman and girl

give them the same opportunities...

the world gets better for...

ALL

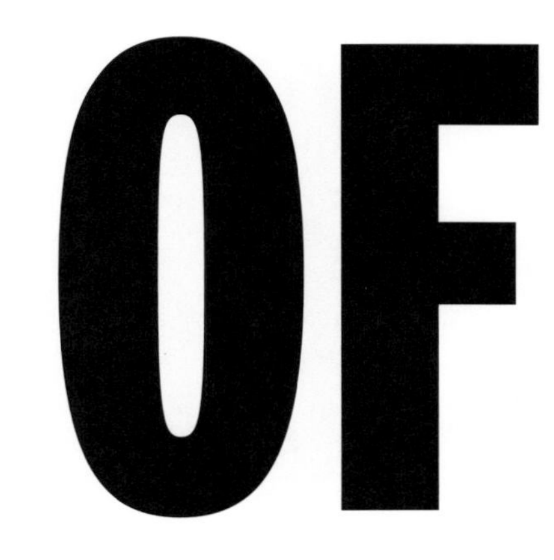
OF

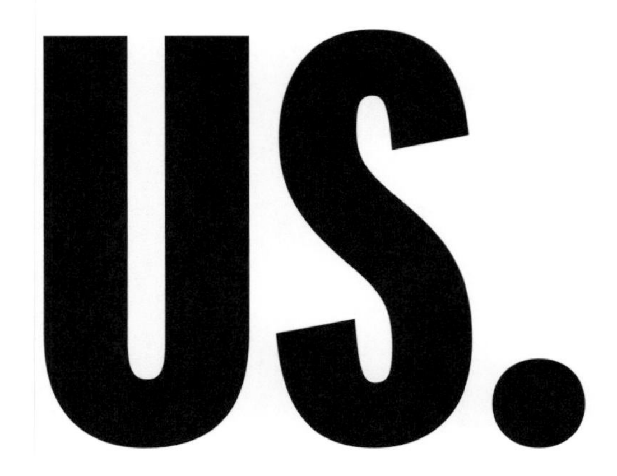
US.

Outro
for grownups

All right, that was pretty intense, huh? Good, because fighting for everyone to have the same opportunities is a PRETTY INTENSE matter.

Everyone is equal, so everyone should have the same opportunities. And if you believe that, guess what?

YOU'RE A FEMINIST!

I'd like to be the first to welcome you and that kiddo with you to the club.

You are a part of a movement that's made up of fellow rascals, rule breakers, think-out-of-the-boxers, and world changers. The only criteria for belonging? Believe that everyone is equal, no matter what their gender is.

Whatever you do, don't let that belief stop with this book. Bring it with you everywhere you go, because you know the same thing I do: being a feminist is super important.

About The Author

Emma Mcilroy (she/her) is the cofounder and CEO of Wildfang, a fashion brand born in a studio apartment in Portland, Oregon, to rethink gender norms and how they show up in our clothing. Together, Emma and Wildfang have given back over $1 million to nonprofits focused on women's rights, racial justice, and LGBTQ+ rights.

Emma has been named one of Inc.'s Female Founders 100, Oregon Entrepreneur of the Year, a Henry Crown Fellow from the Aspen Institute, and her "Yeah, Maybe" TEDx talk has racked up over 100k views. When she's not running a startup, Emma can be found playing, coaching, or watching sports, likely Rory McIlroy or Liverpool FC.

She wrote this book to empower kids to become the best possible version of themselves, and to smash gender norms and the patriarchy in the process.

 @irishem333  @emmamcilroy1983